Cambodian NEW YEAR

by Michèle Dufresne

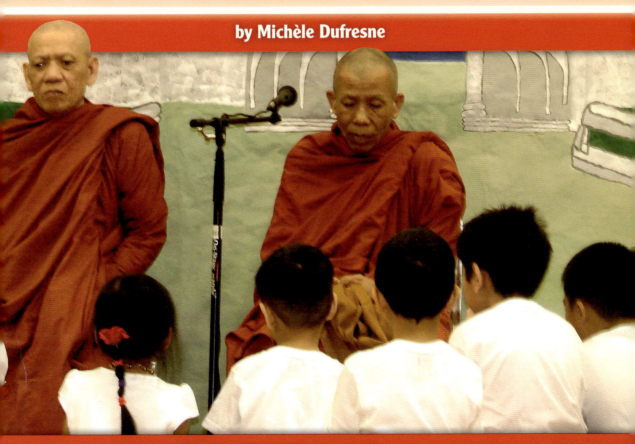

Pioneer Valley Educational Press, Inc.

TABLE OF CONTENTS

American Cambodian School............................ 4

Cambodia.. 8

Preparing for the Celebration 10

The Cambodian New Year 16

Glossary 24

Index... 24

AMERICAN CAMBODIAN SCHOOL

Hi! My name is Mardi.

Every Wednesday after school,
I go to an American Cambodian School.

I am learning to read and write in **Khmer**.
Khmer is the language spoken in Cambodia.
I am proud of myself.
I can speak, read, and write
in two languages: English and Khmer.

៦០/១០

ម៉ា វ៉ា ន៊ូ   ក ខ គ ឃ ង
ម៉ា វ៉ា ន៊ូ   ច ឆ ជ ឈ ញ
ម៉ា វ៉ា ន៊ូ   ដ ឋ ឌ ឍ
ម៉ា វ៉ា ន៊ូ   ណ ត ថ ទ ធ ន
ម៉ា វ៉ា ន៊ូ

ខ្ញុំស្គាល់

CAMBODIA

Cambodia is a country in Southeast Asia.

The Cambodian New Year is in April. April is the first month of the year in the Cambodian calendar. It is also the end of the growing season. In Cambodia, this is the time to relax and enjoy the food that was grown.

PREPARING FOR THE CELEBRATION

Soon we will celebrate
the Cambodian New Year.
The Cambodian New Year is a special holiday.
I am very excited!

We are going to put on a special show
for all the boys and girls at my school.
My friends and I will practice for many weeks
to learn Cambodian dances.
My Khmer teacher is helping us.

At school, we are celebrating the Cambodian New Year. To get ready for the celebration, we brought in special things from home.

I brought in a doll made in Cambodia. The doll is dressed in **traditional** clothes. Everyone stops to look at my doll in the display case.

Special food will be prepared
for the celebration.
There will be many of the traditional foods
of Cambodia. I can't wait!

THE CAMBODIAN NEW YEAR

The Cambodian New Year celebration
will last for three days.

On the first day of the New Year celebration,
the monks from the Buddhist temple come
to watch us dance and sing.
They start the celebration with a prayer.

The New Year celebration is a time
to show respect for **elders**,
including grandparents, parents, and teachers.

Our families and the children and teachers from my school also come to watch us.

We begin with the Angel Dance. This traditional dance is about a **guardian** angel who comes to bless the new year.

We also do the Coconut Dance.

Then we act out some scenes from life in Cambodia.

The New Year celebration will last for two more days. There will be visits to the Buddhist temple to bring the monks food and to pray for dead **ancestors**. There will also be Khmer music, dancing, and games.

At the end of our program, we sing a New Year's song. We say Happy New Year in Khmer to our friends and family: "Sur sdey chnam thmey" (*SOO-ur sah'DAY chah'NAHM tah'MAY*).

GLOSSARY

ancestors: the people from whom someone is descended

elder: an older person

guardian: one who watches over someone or something

Khmer: the language spoken in Cambodia

traditional: part of the culture, passed from generation to generation

INDEX

American Cambodian School 4
ancestors 22
Angel Dance 18
Cambodia 6, 8, 12, 14, 20
Cambodian New Year 8, 10, 12, 16
Cambodian sweet and sour soup 15
celebration 10, 12, 14, 16, 22
Coconut Dance 20
dance 10, 16, 18, 20, 22
egg rolls 15

elder 16
food 8, 14, 22
fried rice 15
guardian 18
Khmer 6, 10, 22
languages 6
traditional 12, 14, 18
sing 16, 22
Southeast Asia 8
stir fried clear noodles 15